1942

The German V-2 rocket is the first object to escape Earth's gravity and reach space.

2009

Some raindrops are found to fall faster than terminal velocity—which shouldn't be possible.

1919

Arthur Eddington proves Einstein right by showing light bends around the Sun.

1969

Neil Armstrong becomes the first person to experience a different gravity than Earth's as he walks on the moon.

1957

Sputnik becomes the first artificial satellite to orbit Earth.

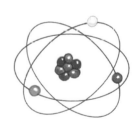

1927

Georges Lemaître proposes the Big Bang theory.

1998

Scientists suggest dark energy works against gravity, pushing matter farther apart and expanding the universe.

Can We See Gravity?

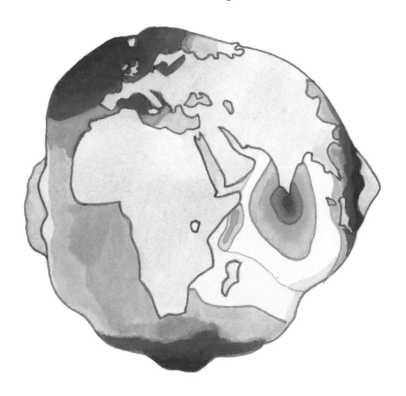

Earth has a slightly strange shape. It's not exactly a sphere, because it bulges outward in the middle. It is wider going around the equator than it is going from pole to pole. This funny shape is called an oblate spheroid.

Besides having an unusual shape, Earth is not the same density all over, and it has an uneven surface. This means that there is uneven gravity over Earth's surface. Scientists have measured this and created a map to show the results. This gravity map of Earth is known as the "Potsdam potato," because it looks a bit like a potato, and because the group of scientists who study it are based in Potsdam, Germany.

On the map, the red areas indicate the highest levels of gravity, and the light blue areas show where gravity levels are lowest.

Author:

Anne Rooney studied English at Cambridge University, England, and then earned a Ph.D. at Cambridge. She has held teaching posts at several UK universities and is currently a Royal Literary Fund fellow at Newnham College, Cambridge. She has written more than 150 books for children and adults, including several on the history of science and medicine. She also writes children's fiction.

Artist:

Mark Bergin was born in Hastings, England, in 1961. He studied at Eastbourne College of Art and specializes in historical reconstructions, aviation, and maritime subjects. He lives in Bexhill-on-Sea with his wife and children.

Series creator:

David Salariya was born in Dundee, Scotland. He has illustrated a wide range of books and has created and designed many new series for publishers in the UK and overseas. David established The Salariya Book Company in 1989. He lives in Brighton, England, with his wife, illustrator Shirley Willis, and their son, Jonathan.

Editor: **Jacqueline Ford**

Editorial Assistant: **Mark Williams**

Published in Great Britain in 2016 by
The Salariya Book Company Ltd
25 Marlborough Place, Brighton BN1 1UB

ISBN-13: 978-0-531-21487-9 (lib. bdg.) 978-0-531-22437-3 (pbk.)

All rights reserved.
Published in 2016 in the United States
by Franklin Watts
An imprint of Scholastic Inc.

A CIP catalog record for this book is available from the Library of Congress.

Printed and bound in China.
Printed on paper from sustainable sources.

1 2 3 4 5 6 7 8 9 10 R 25 24 23 22 21 20 19 18 17 16

PAPER FROM
SUSTAINABLE
FORESTS

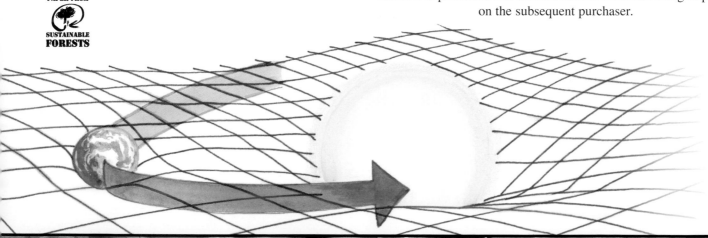

You Wouldn't Want to Live Without™
Gravity!

Written by
Anne Rooney

Illustrated by
Mark Bergin

Series created by
David Salariya

Franklin Watts®
An Imprint of Scholastic Inc.

Contents

Introduction

Imagine living without gravity. What would it be like if you couldn't play ball games or jump into a swimming pool, or if you couldn't even sit down? We don't really get a choice about gravity. If you live on Earth, you're going to have to live with gravity. In fact, Earth wouldn't even be here without gravity, and you wouldn't either.

Gravity can be a pain. If it didn't exist, we would never get hurt by falling down, or by things falling on us. But it does a lot of really useful things, too—such as keeping us on Earth and holding the entire universe together! You wouldn't want to live without it.

EVERY TIME you jump, gravity brings you crashing back down to Earth. On a trampoline, there's enough force in the "bounce" to push you back up—briefly.

What Did Gravity Ever Do for You?

Gravity acts a bit like invisible glue, holding everything onto the surface of Earth. It doesn't work only at the surface and on solid things. It holds the ocean down and keeps the air from floating away into space. It even holds the entire Earth itself together as a big blob of spherical planet.

If Earth's gravity suddenly turned off (but don't worry, it won't), everything would whiz off the surface of the planet. All the water, air, people, animals, and objects would go hurtling into space. It might seem fun for a moment, but it really wouldn't be very nice.

WEIGHT IS the effect of gravity pulling mass down toward Earth. On a planet with different gravity, you would have a different weight, but still the same mass.

WITHOUT GRAVITY, nothing would stay in place unless it was tied down. If you tried to pour a drink, the liquid would drift away or stay in the bottle, since there'd be no gravity to make it come out.

GRAVITY CAN be fun. Without it, there would be no roller-coaster rides, and you wouldn't be able to go skiing or sledding, because these all rely on gravity pulling you down when you're up.

Top Tip

Gravity isn't going to turn off, so protect yourself from its more dangerous moments! Wear a helmet when you ride your bike and protective pads if you go skateboarding or roller-skating.

GRAVITY CAN also hurt. With no gravity, you wouldn't fall down stairs or off a bike. Falling is the result of gravity acting on your mass to pull you toward the center of Earth.

WHENEVER ANYTHING falls on you, gravity's to blame for it dropping, and for it hurting if it's heavy. And without gravity, you couldn't drop trash in waste baskets—it would just float around.

GRAVITY ALSO holds the planets in orbit around the Sun, and keeps the moon in orbit around Earth. Without it, the moon and the planets would just wander off into space.

It Started With a Bang!

Where did gravity come from? Very early in the history of the universe, the first particles formed. They started to clump together as gravity attracted them to one another. It seems gravity just emerged once there was matter. The clumps got bigger and bigger—but not quickly! After more than half a billion years, the clumps were big enough to become vast gas clouds that finally led to the formation of galaxies. Stars formed in those galaxies, with systems of planets around some. As the driving force behind all of it, gravity had a lot to do!

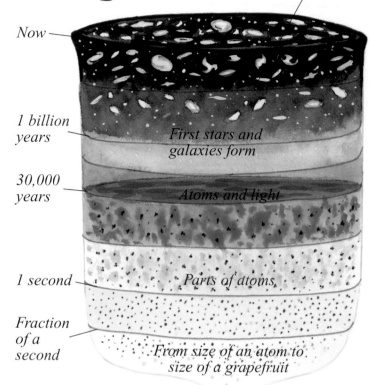

Galaxies form clusters

Now

1 billion years — First stars and galaxies form

30,000 years — Atoms and light

1 second — Parts of atoms

Fraction of a second — From size of an atom to size of a grapefruit

Big Bang

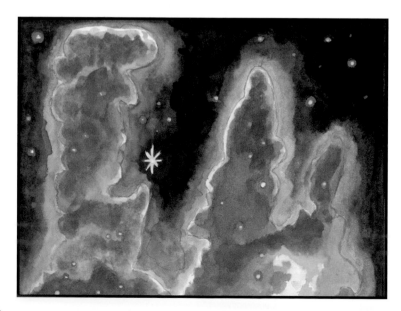

THE BIG BANG theory was first suggested by Belgian priest Georges Lamaître in 1927. It explains how the universe came into existence by expanding rapidly from a tiny single point. All matter and energy rushed outward from the center, and it is still hurtling farther apart today. At the same time, gravity makes it clump together, so the universe is a bit lumpy!

HUGE, TOWERING columns of gas and dust eventually collapsed into stars as gravity pulled matter closer and closer together. Without gravity, the stars would never have formed.

SPINNING CLUMPS of dust and gas formed stars, and matter whirling around them gradually grouped into planets.

IF CHUNKS of matter crashed into each other or drifted too close, they could either be blasted to pieces or joined together to make a bigger chunk.

Name	Solar orbit	Round	Cleared orbit	Planet?
Venus	✔	✔	✔	😊
Earth	✔	✔	✔	😊
Pluto	✔	✔		😟
Haumea	✔		✔	😟

THE RINGS of fine dust around the planet Jupiter have empty spaces between them. These might have been cleared by moons altering the orbit of dust particles with their own gravity.

A PLANET bigger than about 250 miles (400 km) across will become round as gravity pulls in all the corners and bumps. Any smaller, and it may look like a giant potato, with too little gravity to become round.

TO EARN its badge as a planet, a body must (1) be in orbit around the Sun, (2) be large enough to have become round, and (3) have cleared any other matter from its orbit, or adopted it as a moon.

How Fast Will You Fall?

IN 1971, astronaut David Scott traveled to the moon on *Apollo 15*. Once there, he finally tested Galileo's theory: He dropped a hammer and a feather at the same time, and both of them hit the ground together.

talian scientist Galileo Galilei was very interested in gravity. In the 1580s, he suggested that gravity acts in the same way on all falling objects. This is called the law of falling bodies. It means that heavy objects shouldn't fall any faster than light objects if only the effect of gravity is taken into account. But on Earth, air slows falling objects. The shape and mass of an object control how much it is slowed by air resistance as it falls.

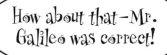

How about that—Mr. Galileo was correct!

GALILEO SAID that if he could drop a bit of wool and a lump of lead without air slowing them down, they would fall at the same rate. He was unable to try it, because there is air everywhere on Earth.

GALILEO experimented with gravity by rolling balls down a slope. He measured how long it took heavy and light balls to reach the bottom and showed that gravity acts in the same way on both—they took the same amount of time.

WHEN THINGS fall through air, eventually the air resistance (air pushing upward) becomes equal to gravity pulling downward. The object stops accelerating and keeps on falling at the same speed, known as terminal velocity. A skydiver falls very fast under gravity at first, then uses a parachute to slow down using air resistance.

WHEN YOU throw a ball, you judge the direction and force of your throw based on the idea of trajectory—all without even thinking about it!

How It Works

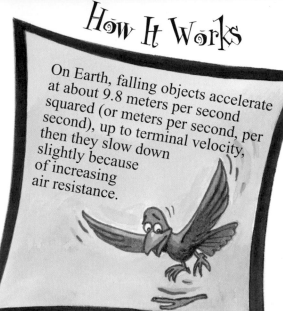

On Earth, falling objects accelerate at about 9.8 meters per second squared (or meters per second, per second), up to terminal velocity, then they slow down slightly because of increasing air resistance.

ASTRONAUT ALAN Shepard struck two golf balls on the moon. With no air resistance and little gravity, he reported they went for "miles and miles."

THE FLIGHT path of a cannonball or arrow is called its trajectory. Firing it gives it a push that launches it. As it flies, gravity continually pulls on it and the object falls to Earth.

Fore!

What Did the Apple Do to Newton?

NEWTON WAS interested in the motion of the moon and planets, which he studied with a telescope. He finally realized that the gravity of the Sun and the planets controlled their orbits.

People long ago were interested in why things fell to Earth, but Isaac Newton was the first person to investigate it carefully. He saw gravity as a force that pulls objects together. Gravity acts on and between all objects. The strength of the force of gravity depends on how much mass each object has, and how far apart the objects are. The force of gravity between objects decreases as they move apart.

AFTER SEEING an apple fall from a tree in 1666, Newton came up with the idea that gravity holds the moon in orbit around Earth. If gravity could pull an apple to Earth, why not the moon, too?

NEWTON EXPLAINED the orbits of the planets around the Sun in terms of gravity. The Sun's gravity pulls on the planets, so they can't escape. Some orbits are a bit wobbly—that's because other nearby planets and moons can pull on them a bit with their own gravity.

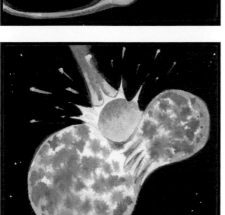

THE MOON is thought to be made up of debris that resulted when Earth collided with a giant asteroid or another planet billions of years ago. The debris from the collision was held in orbit by Earth's gravity, and its own gravity brought the chunks together. Spinning around, all parts of the new moon were pulled toward the center by its gravity. This is how all planets become round.

THE MOON'S gravity causes the tides on Earth. As the moon goes around Earth, it pulls the water of the oceans with it so that the water bulges out.

We have gravity to thank for these waves!

ALL OBJECTS—even atoms—exert a gravitational force, but it's so tiny we don't notice any effect from it. Even you exert your own personal gravity!

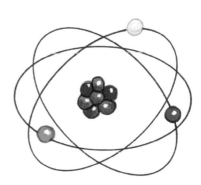

IF EVERYONE stood on the same side of Earth, the center of its gravitational force would shift. Gravity is centered where the mass of the planet is centered, and this would change if we all grouped together.

Why Is Gravity Like a Hole?

Newton's theory of gravity as a force was accepted for more than 200 years. It was pretty good at explaining why the moon goes around Earth and why apples fall to the ground, but it didn't work on very tiny or very large scales. In 1666, that didn't matter, since no one knew about really tiny things like atoms and really big things like galaxies.

But Albert Einstein didn't agree that gravity is a force. In 1915, he described it as disturbance in space. A large body, such as a star, makes something like a "dip" that lighter objects fall toward. You could think of it as being a bit like a heavy ball making a dip in a blanket pulled taut.

GRAVITY AND acceleration are basically the same thing. They are both measured in meters per second squared (or meters per second, per second), which means that the speed increases each second. So if gravity pulls a rock down a hill when you are nearby—run!

SPACE-TIME isn't really like a blanket, which is just a surface. It has four dimensions, with all dimensions dipping in toward the heavy object.

Experiment with a blanket held taut and some balls to see how curved space-time makes objects gather together.

IN HIS General Theory of Relativity, Einstein explained gravity as distorting space-time—the combination of space and time that makes the fabric of the universe. A heavy object like a star warps space-time, pulling other objects in.

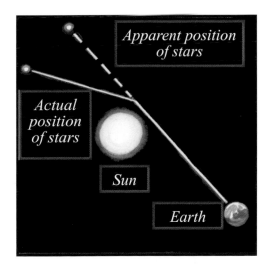

Apparent position of stars

Actual position of stars

Sun

Earth

EINSTEIN BELIEVED light could be bent by the gravity of massive stars. If light curves around something in front of it, that makes it possible to see things that should be hidden.

TO TEST Einstein's theory, the astronomer Arthur Eddington sailed to East Africa in 1919 to watch and photograph an eclipse and see what lay directly behind the Sun.

WHEN THESE eclipse photos were compared with one taken at night, it showed that the position of a star cluster near the Sun didn't match. This proved that light from the stars was bent around the Sun.

Putting Gravity to Work

Gravity is always there; it's never turned off, it needs no power source, and it costs nothing. So it's smart to put it to work. We make gravity work for us in lots of different ways.

People were making use of gravity long before anyone understood how it works. They exploited gravity's favorite trick of making things fall down. But they also used it to make sure surfaces were perfectly horizontal or vertical, and to measure time. Nowadays we even use it to direct spacecraft.

HAVE YOU ever seen bumpy or slanting water? No. Water will always form a smooth horizontal surface. This means it can be used to show whether or not a surface is flat; simply place a bowl of water on the surface and see if the water is at the same level all around the sides. If not, the surface isn't flat. Easy!

GRAVITY MAKES a weighted string hang straight down. So by making a plumb line—a cord attached to a weight—we can check to make sure verticals are straight.

That works really well!

BEFORE CLOCKS were invented, hourglasses were used as a way to measure time. An hourglass depends on gravity, because it works by sand falling steadily through a small hole as it flows from the top of the glass to the bottom. It takes exactly the same amount of time for the sand to fall every time the hourglass is turned over, which means it is a reliable way to measure time.

You Can Do It!

Make your own plumb line by tying something fairly heavy to a piece of thread or thin string. Use it to check how straight and vertical some of the things around you are. How straight is your door? Or that jungle gym?

A WATER mill harnesses the force of falling water, using it to turn a wheel. The wheel turns an axle which drives machinery. The mechanical power can be used to grind corn.

A HYDROELECTRIC dam also uses the power of falling water. But it's much bigger than a water mill! A huge cascade of water drives machinery that generates electricity from the waterfall's power. Electricity from gravity!

EARTH'S GRAVITY isn't the only gravity we use. Spacecraft boost their speed with a gravity-assist maneuver using the gravity of another planet as a slingshot. Gravity pulls the spacecraft in, making it go faster and faster, and then it speeds by the planet, changing direction slightly but keeping its speed.

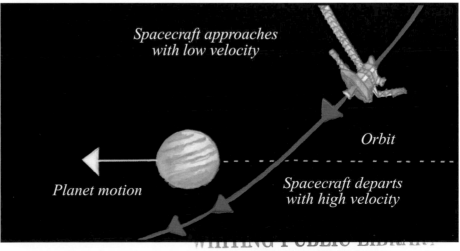

Spacecraft approaches with low velocity

Orbit

Planet motion

Spacecraft departs with high velocity

What Goes Up But Doesn't Come Down?

One of the ways we put gravity to work is keeping satellites in orbit above us. A satellite is anything that is in orbit around a planet. The moon is our only natural satellite, and it has been orbiting Earth for about 4.5 billion years without ever falling down.

We now have thousands of human-made satellites as well. They have all been carried into orbit by rockets and released at just the right height. They do lots of different types of work. Like the moon, they are kept in their place by gravity. Without gravity, we couldn't have satellite TV, cell phones, or GPS!

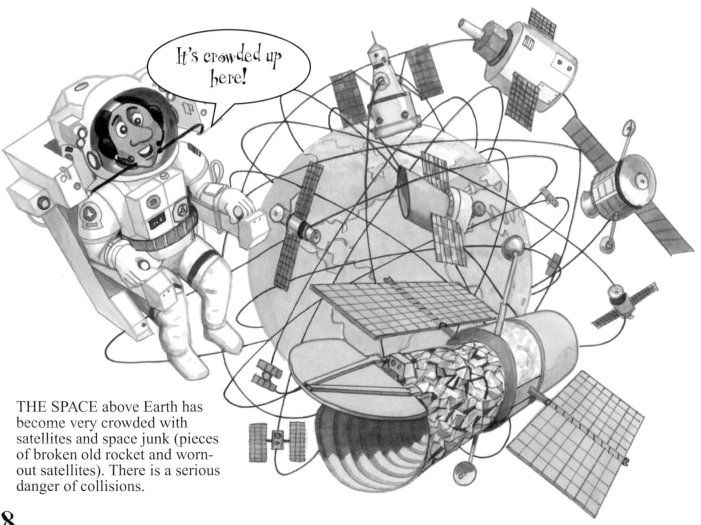

It's crowded up here!

THE SPACE above Earth has become very crowded with satellites and space junk (pieces of broken old rocket and worn-out satellites). There is a serious danger of collisions.

A SATELLITE'S speed must be carefully matched to its altitude so that it stays in orbit. When dropped in space, a satellite continues to travel at the same speed and altitude as the rocket that released it. If it slows and starts to fall, it will usually burn up in Earth's atmosphere. If it goes too fast, it will whiz off into space.

SATELLITES HAVE lots of different jobs. We use them for telecommunications, weather, and spying, as astronomical telescopes, for Google Earth, GPS—even measuring gravity!

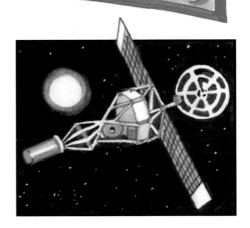

NOT ALL satellites orbit Earth. Some old spaceships are in orbit around the Sun, held in place by the Sun's gravity.

SATELLITE ORBITS do slowly decay. Most satellites burn up in the atmosphere as they fall, but occasionally chunks may fall to Earth.

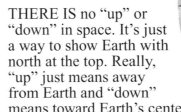

THERE IS no "up" or "down" in space. It's just a way to show Earth with north at the top. Really, "up" just means away from Earth and "down" means toward Earth's center.

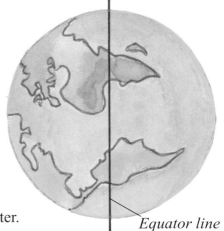

Equator line

19

Your Body Loves Gravity

Your body has evolved to live with Earth's gravity. Either more or less gravity wouldn't be good for it. NASA has to think about this when planning long spaceflights, especially when considering the possibility of people living on other planets or moons or on space stations. On a trip to and from Mars, astronauts would spend more than 14 months in space without the effects of gravity.

ON A SPACEFLIGHT, astronauts experience weightlessness. Their bones and muscles don't have to do any work or push against gravity to keep their bodies upright, and this is really not very healthy. Bodies behave best when they have work to do. That's why exercise is good for you. Many parts of the body can suffer without gravity.

Stomach

Ears

Arm bones

Spine

Leg muscles

BONES LOSE some density when there is less or no gravity, so after a long flight, astronauts can have fragile bones that break more easily. They can lose 1 percent of bone mass each month, up to more than half of the total bone density. An astronaut with broken legs couldn't explore a planet very well.

WEIGHTLESSNESS CAUSES space sickness. The zero-gravity training module is even called the "vomit comet" by astronauts because it makes everyone sick!

JELLYFISH HAVE tiny crystals in their bodies that move under gravity and help the jellyfish tell which way is up. In space, these don't work. Jellyfish born in space can't cope when they are back on Earth.

MUSCLES ALSO weaken on a long spaceflight. They can waste at a rate of 5 percent a week if not used to push against gravity. Astronauts build muscle with exercise before long spaceflights.

HUMANS BALANCE using fluid and tiny hairs deep inside the ears. If a baby was born on a long spaceflight, could it balance when it first encountered gravity on a planet? We don't know!

Too Much of a Good Thing?

IT WOULD be hard work moving around on a planet with stronger gravity, and the atmosphere would push down on you, too.

If too little gravity is bad for you, what about a bit more than we're used to? If astronauts ever start visiting other planets, some planets will have less gravity than Earth, but some might have more. Great explorers can't be too fussy about gravity.

The strength of a planet's gravity depends on its size and density (measured as mass in grams per cubic centimeter of planet). Within the solar system, the moon has 17 percent of Earth's gravity, Mars has just over a third (37 percent), and the gas giant Jupiter has more than twice Earth's gravity. Jupiter doesn't have a solid surface, but astronauts would be tugged strongly inward toward the center. Outside our solar system, who knows what we might find?

AS GRAVITY pulls down on your body, it squishes the spongy discs in your spine and you get shorter during the day, even on Earth. If there were stronger gravity on Earth, you would be shorter all the time.

ON A PLANET with stronger gravity, the air would weigh heavily on you. It would be pulled downward with more force, so it would exert more pressure on your body. That would make it harder to move. It would be very tiring.

You Can Do It!

Put on weights and exercise or run. It's much harder work than without weights. That's how hard it would be to live with more gravity—but you wouldn't be able to put down the weights!

YOU WOULD have a gray face like a zombie from a movie, since your blood would tend to be dragged toward the lower part of your body. It would take a lot more work for your heart to keep your blood flowing properly.

DANGER!
BLACK HOLE
DO NOT ENTER

THERE IS a huge amount of gravity in a black hole. A black hole is matter so dense it has collapsed in on itself. It has not lost any of its original mass—it's just squashed into a tiny space. A black hole with the mass of a planet would fit on a teaspoon.

THINGS THAT stray too near a black hole are "spaghettified"— stretched to an incredibly long, thin strip as gravity pulls harder on the closest end than on the farthest end. The long, thin object is then sucked in and completely crushed by the black hole's gravity. There's no escaping it!

Life Without Gravity

Astronauts in space have to live with weightlessness, meaning that they and all their things float around inside the spaceship. They have to do lots of tasks and activities in special ways.

When astronauts are in orbit around Earth, the spacecraft and the astronauts are in free fall, so this makes them weightless—it seems as though there is no gravity. Free fall means that the craft and all its contents are constantly falling toward Earth, pulled by gravity. But at the same time, the speed of the spacecraft means they never actually fall down. Imagine a split second in midair when you jump—and then extend it for weeks or months! That's what living in space is like.

ASTRONAUTS USE special coffee cups shaped like the wing of an airplane. The coffee creeps up the cup on its own, which is good, since tipping it will have no effect!

IT MIGHT seem fun to not need to put things down—you can just leave them in midair. But they easily drift away with the slightest breeze. Everything has to be fastened down.

IF YOU BRUSHED your teeth in space, toothpaste and water would float away! Astronauts learn how to brush without this happening. There are special arrangements to go to the bathroom, too.

You Can Do It!

On Earth, gravity can help save your life. If you get caught in an avalanche and can't tell which way is up, pee or spit. The liquid will travel downward, so you should dig in the opposite direction.

IN WEIGHTLESS conditions, everything floats around—astronauts, objects, food, and drink. It's a struggle to keep track of everything.

EVERYONE'S HAIR looks a mess in space. If your hair normally lies flat, it is only because of gravity. Astronauts have to put up with bad hair days every single day!

ASTRONAUTS DON'T lie down to sleep, because there is no difference between lying down and standing up. To keep from floating away during sleep, they snuggle into a sleeping bag attached to the spaceship wall.

BALL GAMES would be difficult, because the balls would never fall down when thrown. Soon, they would all be floating around the ceiling—although since there's no "up," there's no ceiling either!

Fighting Back

There are some things we do that defy gravity: flying in a plane, spaceflight—even jumping or throwing a ball into the air. If gravity holds us down on Earth, how does anything take off? If we think of gravity as a force, just as Newton did, we can work against it using a stronger force operating in the opposite direction—up! So by giving something a big enough push, we can launch it from the ground, and even into space if the push is big enough.

YOU USE the power of your muscles to exert enough force to push you off the ground when you jump. You even use it to pick your feet up to walk.

ALL KINDS of things can battle gravity long enough to get airborne—even a tiny insect. Only spacecraft can escape gravity for good, though.

We're defying gravity!

Fast moving air (low pressure)

Thrust

Lift

Slower moving air (higher pressure)

PLANES TAKE off by going very fast but are held up by "lift" from air beneath that counteracts gravity.

How It Works

Movement is ruled by forces. A push or pull in one direction will move an object until a force changes or stops it. Movement away from Earth is always countered by gravity pulling things down toward Earth.

BIRDS PUSH air down with their wings. That creates pressure below that holds them up.

THE THRUST from powerful rocket engines produces enough force pushing downward to force the rocket up, overcoming gravity. With enough force, it can escape into space.

LEAVES, SEEDS, and insects are so light they are easily carried by the wind.

IT TAKES more energy to escape the Sun's gravity than Earth's gravity. So a rocket with enough energy to escape Earth can be dragged toward the Sun.

A HELIUM balloon is filled with gas lighter than air. It goes up because the heavier air falls down around it. Gravity still acts on the balloon, but not as strongly as on the air.

So, Could You Live Without Gravity?

Living without gravity might be fun for a brief exploration, which you could do in a spaceship—but you wouldn't want to do it forever. If gravity disappeared, we'd all die. But if humans ever colonize space, living with different amounts of gravity is something we'll have to think about. If we go outside our solar system, we might find planets with a great deal more gravity than Earth, as well as planets with less gravity. That would be a struggle to get used to, especially after a long period of weightlessness on the journey there. Once you've lived with gravity, you wouldn't want to live without it!

IF YOU went to live on a planet with more gravity (but not too much more) than ours, your body would adapt eventually. At first, though, it would be exhausting. It would be like training to be a superathlete, because you'd need better muscles and a stronger heart and bones.

IF YOU went to live on a planet with much less gravity than ours, you probably wouldn't be able to come back. You might be able to build up your muscles again, but your bones would be very weak. So make sure it's a lovely planet before you go!

IF WE colonized planets with much more gravity than Earth, we would need to find ways of overcoming the extra pull on our bodies. Perhaps we could devise a special antigravity outfit? Jet-propelled boots might help us to move around more easily!

Top Tip

If you think you might have to go on a trip to a planet with low gravity, pack a very heavy outfit. It will help to keep you grounded.

OR MAYBE we could just live on the highest places where the gravity is lowest. The farther you go from the surface of a planet, the weaker the force of gravity becomes. Even on Earth, if you climb to the top of a high mountain, gravity is slightly less than it is at sea level. You weigh a tiny bit less at the top of a mountain. On a planet with lots of gravity, being high up could make a slight difference.

IDEALLY, WE need to find a planet that has not too much gravity and not too little gravity—a "Goldilocks" planet that's just right for our bodies. A planet just like Earth, in fact. Luckily, we already have one!

29

Glossary

Accelerate To go faster and faster.

Air resistance The force of air acting against a falling or moving object.

Asteroid A chunk of rock and/or ice that travels through space.

Atom A very tiny particle of matter; the smallest part that can be identified as one of the chemical elements.

Avalanche A large amount of snow falling or sliding down a mountain; similar to a landslide but with snow instead of rocks and soil.

Axle The rod on which wheels are fixed and rotate.

Big Bang The beginning of the universe, when all matter expanded from an infinitely small point and space-time began.

Decay (orbit) The slowing of an object in orbit so that it begins to fall toward Earth.

Dense Packing a lot of mass into a small volume.

Force A push or pull operating on matter.

Free fall The state of constant falling but never landing.

GPS Global positioning system: a system for measuring exact locations on Earth by referring to the position of satellites in orbit.

Gravity The mechanism that brings bodies with mass together.

Gravity assist A maneuver that involves using the gravity of a planet or moon like a slingshot to accelerate a spacecraft as it passes.

Helium A very light gas that is less dense than air.

Hydroelectric dam A system that captures the energy of a large body of falling water to produce electricity.

Lift The force that pushes an aircraft upward, created by differences in pressure above and below the wings.

Mass The quality of matter that makes it difficult to move or to stop it moving.

Orbit A circular path of an object around a planet, star, or moon that maintains the same height and speed, at the point where gravity is not strong enough to pull the object downward.

Plumb line A tool that uses a weight on the end of a cord to indicate a perfectly vertical line.

Satellite An object in orbit around another body (often around Earth).

Solar System The system of Sun, planets, moons, comets, asteroids, and other bodies within the range of the Sun's gravity.

Space-time The combination of interlinked space and time in which the universe exists.

Telecommunications Communication methods that operate over a distance using electromagnetic radiation such as light and radio waves.

Terminal velocity The fastest speed a falling object can achieve under gravity.

Trajectory The path followed by an object that is thrown, fired, or otherwise propelled.

Weight The operation of gravity on mass.

Weightlessness The sensation of having no weight experienced by astronauts in free fall while in orbit.

Zero gravity Condition in which an object is free-falling with no resistance.

Index

A
acceleration 14
air resistance 10, 11
astronaut 10, 11, 20, 21, 22, 23, 24
atom 14

B
balloon 27
Big Bang 8
black hole 23
body 20, 21, 22
bones 21

D
density 22
dust clouds 8, 9

E
eclipse 15
Eddington, Arthur 15
Einstein, Albert 14, 15
electricity 17
exercise 20

F
force 12, 26
free fall 21, 24

G
galaxy 14
Galileo Galilei 10, 11
gas clouds 8, 9
General Theory of Relativity 15
gravity-assist maneuver 17

H
hourglass 17
hydroelectric dam 17

I
International Space Station 19

J
jellyfish 21
jump 5, 26
Jupiter 9, 22

L
Lamaître, Georges 8
law of falling bodies 10
light 15

M
Mars 22
mass 6, 10
moon 7, 12, 13, 14, 18, 22
muscle 21

N
NASA 20
Newton, Isaac 12, 13, 14, 26

O
orbit 9, 12, 13, 18, 19

P
plane 27
planet 9, 12, 13, 17, 18, 22, 28
plumb line 16

R
rings of Jupiter 9
rocket 27
roller coaster 6

S
satellite 18, 19
Scott, David 10
Shepard, Alan 11
skydiver 11
space junk 18
spaceship 18, 19
space sickness 21
space-time 14, 15
spaghettification 23
star 8, 9, 15
Sun 7, 12, 13, 15, 19, 27

T
terminal velocity 11
thrust 27
tide 13

V
vomit comet 21

W
water 16, 17
water mill 17
weight 6
weightlessness 20, 21, 24, 25

Z
zero gravity 21

Top Wacky Facts About Gravity

Objects weigh more at the poles than at the equator, so if you took a 10-pound (4.53 kg) penguin to equatorial Africa, it would weigh 9.91 pounds (4.49 kg). And it would be angry!

Gravity changes depending where you are on Earth. To feel the most effect from gravity, go to Anchorage, Alaska, where it's at its strongest. If you'd rather feel a gentler pull, visit central Africa or India, where gravity is at its least powerful.

At the very edge of the atmosphere, gravity is not strong enough to hold gas molecules in place. This means that bits of our atmosphere are constantly escaping into space. Small moons and planets don't have enough gravity to hold onto an atmosphere at all.

- Even 62 miles (100 km) above Earth, gravity is still only 3 percent less than it is at Earth's surface. You would have to go a very long way to escape Earth's gravity completely.

- In activities such as drag racing, stunt flying (acrobatics in planes), and space training, people experience many times the acceleration of normal gravity (1 g). The highest g-force anyone has voluntarily experienced is 83 g for 0.04 of a second—by Captain Eli L. Beeding, who experimented with human endurance of g-force for the U.S. Air Force.

- Astronauts in *Apollo 8* used Silly Putty to keep their tools in one place and stop them from drifting around the spacecraft.

Did You Know?

We tend to use "weight" and "mass" to mean the same thing. But actually they are different. Mass measures how difficult it is to get something moving or stop it moving. Even in zero gravity, it takes effort to make a stationary thing move.

Weight measures the impact gravity has on something, so it varies with different amounts of gravity. On planets with stronger or weaker gravity, your mass would be the same, but your weight would be different.

Figure out how much you would weigh on another planet. For each 10 pounds of your weight, multiply it by the number in the table for the place in space you'd like to live. For example, if you weigh 90 pounds, your weight on Mercury is 3.7 x 9 = 33.3 pounds.

PLANET OR OTHER BODY	MULTIPLY BY	PLANET OR OTHER BODY	MULTIPLY BY
Mercury	3.7	Saturn	10.6
Venus	9	Uranus	8.8
Mars	3.7	Neptune	11.2
Jupiter	23.6	Pluto	0.6
Moon	1.6	Sun	270.7